Bond

No Nonsense
Maths

10–11 years

Contents

Central pull-out pages

Numbers and place value

ten million	million	hundred thousand	ten thousand	thousands	hundreds	tens	units
1	**0**	**0**	**0**	**0**	**0**	**0**	

Ten million

1. **Write the written number in numerals.**

   a six million, thirty-eight thousand and two _____

   b nine million, one hundred thousand and fifty-five _____

   c three million, five hundred and seventy-seven thousand and eleven _____

   d five million, eight hundred and one thousand, three hundred and sixty _____

   e nine million, nine hundred and ninety-nine thousand, nine hundred and nine _____

2. **What number needs to go in the box?**

   a $2\,678\,450 = 2\,000\,000 + 600\,000 +$ _____ $+ 8\,000 + 400 + 50 + 0$

   b $8\,878\,676 = 8\,000\,000 + 800\,000 + 70\,000 +$ _____ $+ 600 + 70 + 6$

   c $3\,585\,732 =$ _____ $+ 500\,000 + 80\,000 + 5\,000 + 700 + 30 + 2$

   d $9\,999\,999 = 9\,000\,000 + 900\,000 +$ _____ $+ 9\,000 + 900 + 90 + 9$

   e $1\,213\,141 = 1\,000\,000 + 200\,000 + 10\,000 + 3\,000 +$ _____ $+ 40 + 1$

3. **Write these numbers as words.**

   a $4\,323\,675$ _____

   b $308\,004$ _____

   c $7\,004\,399$ _____

4. **Put these numbers in order, largest first.**

   a 100 100   110 011   100 001   1 000 000   11 011

   _____ _____ _____ _____ _____

b 2367451　　　3617423　　　2634751　　　3167243　　　2736541

_____　　　　_____　　　　_____　　　　_____　　　　_____

c 5544662　　　4466552　　　6655442　　　4455662　　　5566442

_____　　　　_____　　　　_____　　　　_____　　　　_____

5. **Add the correct 'more than' (>) or 'less than' (<) sign.**

a 56438 ☐ 56348　　**b** 156839 ☐ 165893　　**c** 33765 ☐ 33675

d 58375 ☐ 58377　　**e** 9867563 ☐ 9876562　　**f** 776777 ☐ 776677

6. **How many more is ...**

a 567342 than 566342? _____　　　　**b** 1765877 than 1765876? _____

c 787865 than 787665? _____　　　　**d** 6574328 than 6374328? _____

0　　Tough	OK	Got it!　26	

Total

☐ 26

Challenge yourself

a Using eight different digits write the largest number you can.　_____

b Now change two of the digits you chose in a. and write the
smallest number you can.　_____

c Write both answers in words.

_____

_____

_____

_____

Number sequences and properties

Look at these number lines.

Rule: **the numbers decrease 15 at a time.**

231	216	201	186	171	156	141	126	111	96

Rule: **the numbers increase 0.5 at a time.**

1·5	2·0	2·5	3·0	3·5	4·0	4·5	5·0	5·5	6·0

1. **What is the rule for each of these number lines?**

a

208	195	182	169	156	143	130	117	104	91	78

Rule: _____

b

589	564	539	514	489	464	439	414	389	364	339

Rule: _____

c

7·75	7·5	7·25	7	6·75	6·5	6·25	6·0	5·75	5·5	5·25

Rule: _____

2. **Finish these number lines.**

a

−42	−20	2	24	46	68				

b

513	490	467	444	421	398				

c

135	119	103	87	71	55				

d

217	226	235	244	253	262				

There are a few easy rules to help us know whether a whole number is divisible by a certain number. A number is divisible by …

2 if the last digit is even *132*   **3** if the sum of its digits is divisible by 3 *168*
4 if the last two digits are divisible by 4 *112* **5** if the last digit is 0 or 5 *435*
6 if it is even and also divisible by 3 *534* **9** if the sum of its digits is divisible by 9 *135*
10 if the last digit is 0 *890*

3. **Write the number or numbers each of these whole numbers are divisible by.**

a 555 _____

b 356 _____

c 405 _____

d 1 010 _____

e 168 _____

f 237 _____

g 356 _____

h 264 _____

i 2 545 _____

j 6 624 _____

4. **How would you know whether a whole number is divisible by 25?**
Write your own rule.

_____

0			18
Tough	OK	Got it!	

Total

/18

Challenge yourself

These number sequences are more challenging. See whether you can finish them, then explain the rule you used.

a

1	1	2	3	5						

Rule: _____

b

1	2	4	8	16						

Rule: _____

c

1	2	5	14	41						

Rule: _____

5

Addition and subtraction

Do you remember how to do addition and subtraction with bigger numbers?

Here is a reminder …

Addition:

```
  3 5 6 7        3 5 6 7        3 5 6 7        3 5 6 7
+ 4 7 2 4      + 4 7 2 4      + 4 7 2 4      + 4 7 2 4
_____      _____      _____      _____
        1            9 1          2 9 1        8 2 9 1
      1              1          1   1        1   1
```

Subtraction:

```
              4 1            4 1          7 1 4 1        7 1 4 1
  8 2 5 3      8 2 5 3        8 2 5 3      8 2 5 3        8 2 5 3
-   4 4 7    -   4 4 7      -   4 4 7    -   4 4 7      -   4 4 7
_____    _____      _____    _____      _____
                    6              0 6          8 0 6      7 8 0 6
```

---

1. **Complete these additions and subtractions.**

   a
   ```
     7 2 1 9
   + 5 3 2 1
   _____
   ```

   b
   ```
     6 2 1 0
   + 3 3 8 9
   _____
   ```

   c
   ```
     5 4 2 1
   -   7 3 2
   _____
   ```

   d
   ```
     4 4 4 4
   -   5 5 5
   _____
   ```

   e
   ```
     2 1 9 8
   + 3 6 7 5
   _____
   ```

   f
   ```
       7 2 5
   -   6 5 7
   _____
   ```

   g
   ```
     7 1 1 8
   + 1 6 9 2
   _____
   ```

   h
   ```
     2 7 9 6
   + 5 9 8 1
   _____
   ```

   i
   ```
     1 9 2 3
   - 1 0 7 8
   _____
   ```

2. **Now solve these problems. Show your workings.**

   a Hannah thought of a number with four digits.
      Aman said to take 585 from her number.
      Hannah's answer was 4 272.
      What was the number Hannah first started with?

b Mrs Turner won £1 000.
In the first week she spent £459 and in the second week £396.
How much money did she have left for the third week?

_____

c A toy costs £13·80, a T-shirt costs £14·79 and a book costs £5·99.
Is £35·00 enough money to pay for these things?

_____

d A theatre has 2 548 seats.
On Monday 1 259 seats were sold. How many seats were empty?

_____

On Tuesday all but 372 were sold. How many seats were sold?

_____

0	Tough	OK	Got it!	13

Total

13 / 13

Challenge yourself

Look at these digits.   6   9   2   9   7

a Make the largest number you can using these digits. _____

b Make the smallest number you can using these digits. _____

c What is the sum of the two numbers you have made? _____

d What is the difference between the two numbers you have made? _____

Short and long multiplication

Do you remember?

$$
\begin{array}{r}
2\,6 \\
\times\ \ 6 \\
\hline
1\,5\,6 \\
\end{array}
$$
  3

1. Find the answers.

a
$$
\begin{array}{r}
5\,6 \\
\times\ \ 2 \\
\hline
\end{array}
$$

b
$$
\begin{array}{r}
7\,8 \\
\times\ \ 5 \\
\hline
\end{array}
$$

c
$$
\begin{array}{r}
3\,2 \\
\times\ \ 6 \\
\hline
\end{array}
$$

d
$$
\begin{array}{r}
2\,7\,1 \\
\times\ \ \ 7 \\
\hline
\end{array}
$$

e
$$
\begin{array}{r}
1\,6\,3 \\
\times\ \ \ 6 \\
\hline
\end{array}
$$

f
$$
\begin{array}{r}
2\,2\,1 \\
\times\ \ \ 7 \\
\hline
\end{array}
$$

Look at how we do long multiplication.

```
  1 2                        1 2
  1 2 4                      1 2 4
× 2 6                      × 2 6
─────                      ─────
2 4 8 0  (124 × 20)   OR     7 4 4  (124 × 6)
  7 4 4  (124 × 6)         2 4 8 0  (124 × 20)
─────                      ─────
3 2 2 4                    3 2 2 4
─────                      ─────
  1 1                        1 1
```

2. Complete these multiplications.

a
$$
\begin{array}{r}
4\,2\,2 \\
\times\ 2\,3 \\
\hline
\end{array}
$$

b
$$
\begin{array}{r}
5\,2\,1 \\
\times\ 2\,7 \\
\hline
\end{array}
$$

c   1 5 1
   ×   3 1
   ———
   ———

d   2 0 2
   ×   3 4
   ———
   ———

e   1 2 3 5
   ×   4 1
   ———
   ———

f   2 3 5 1
   ×   5 1
   ———
   ———

0 Tough	OK	Got it! 12

Total

/ 12

Challenge yourself

Solve these problems.

a A box contains 235 ice-lollies.
How many ice-lollies will be in 26 boxes? _____

b Cleo the cat eats 42 cans of cat food a month. A can of cat food costs 32p.
How much does Cleo's food cost for a month? _____

c A football sticker book holds 135 stickers.
How many stickers will 25 books hold? _____

Times tables

QUICK TIP!
If you write the answers in pencil you can rub them out and have another go to try to beat your time.

1. **How quickly can you answer these multiplication questions?**

Time yourself. Can you do them all in 30 seconds?

$3 \times 6 =$ _____	$7 \times 7 =$ _____	$12 \times 5 =$ _____
$8 \times 7 =$ _____	$2 \times 8 =$ _____	$4 \times 8 =$ _____
$9 \times 2 =$ _____	$9 \times 6 =$ _____	$11 \times 4 =$ _____
$6 \times 6 =$ _____	$7 \times 6 =$ _____	$3 \times 7 =$ _____
$7 \times 3 =$ _____	$3 \times 3 =$ _____	$9 \times 9 =$ _____
$5 \times 9 =$ _____	$5 \times 8 =$ _____	$1 \times 7 =$ _____
$10 \times 8 =$ _____	$6 \times 9 =$ _____	$9 \times 12 =$ _____
$6 \times 4 =$ _____	$10 \times 4 =$ _____	$5 \times 2 =$ _____
$3 \times 9 =$ _____	$8 \times 8 =$ _____	$11 \times 11 =$ _____
$8 \times 6 =$ _____	$9 \times 0 =$ _____	$6 \times 4 =$ _____
$7 \times 5 =$ _____	$2 \times 7 =$ _____	$4 \times 12 =$ _____
$9 \times 9 =$ _____	$5 \times 5 =$ _____	$3 \times 9 =$ _____
$8 \times 3 =$ _____	$4 \times 7 =$ _____	$7 \times 10 =$ _____
$2 \times 2 =$ _____	$10 \times 10 =$ _____	$5 \times 3 =$ _____
$5 \times 10 =$ _____	$1 \times 1 =$ _____	$11 \times 7 =$ _____
$3 \times 4 =$ _____	$6 \times 5 =$ _____	$12 \times 12 =$ _____

1st attempt ...
How long did it take you? _____ seconds

2nd attempt ...
How long did it take you? _____ seconds

3rd attempt ...
How long did it take you? _____ seconds

2. **Answer these questions.**

   a What are five nines? _____

   b What is 8 times 8? _____

   c What is 3 multiplied by 7? _____

   d What is 4 times 8? _____

   e Multiply seven by nine. _____

   f What are six sixes? _____

   g What is 10 multiplied by 6? _____

   h What are five eights? _____

   i What is 7 multiplied by 8? _____

   j Multiply two by nine. _____

   k What is four multiplied by four? _____

   l Multiply 8 by 12. _____

3. **Fill in the boxes.**

   a 6 × ☐ = 30

   b ☐ × 5 = 45

   c ☐ × 9 = 18

   d 7 × ☐ = 56

   e ☐ × 6 = 42

   f 4 × ☐ = 32

   g ☐ × 7 = 70

   h ☐ × 6 = 48

   i 3 × ☐ = 24

   j ☐ × 9 = 27

   k 9 × ☐ = 81

   l ☐ × 10 = 100

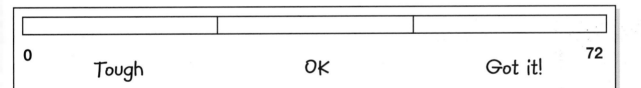

0   Tough   OK   Got it!   72

Total 72

Challenge yourself

Complete the number sentences.

a ☐ × ☐ = 24

b ☐ × ☐ = 54

c ☐ × ☐ = 48

d ☐ × ☐ = 49

e ☐ × ☐ = 2

f ☐ × ☐ = 72

g ☐ × ☐ = 36

h ☐ × ☐ = 18

i ☐ × ☐ = 9

j ☐ × ☐ = 63

Mode, median and mean

To find the mode or median of a set of numbers you need to begin by putting them in order, from smallest to largest.

2   6   3   5   8   6   1   6   7   3   4

This is the same set of numbers in order.

1   2   3   3   4   5   (6   6   6)   7   8

Mode   = the number that appears the **most times** = 6
Median = the number that is in the **middle** of the list = 5

1. **Find the mode and median of these numbers.**
   Remember to put the numbers in order first.

   a   2   3   8   7   3   6   5   3   6

   _2_   _3_   _3_   _3_   _5_   _6_   _6_   _7_   _8_

   Mode = _____   Median = _____

   b   7   1   6   1   4   3   2   1   6

   ____   ____   ____   ____   ____   ____   ____   ____   ____

   Mode = _____   Median = _____

   c   2   5   6   7   2   5   9   3   2

   ____   ____   ____   ____   ____   ____   ____   ____   ____

   Mode = _____   Median = _____

2. **These are the heights in centimetres of 11 children.**
   Find the mode and median.

   137   129   138   136   131   136   131   132   131   139   133

   _129_   _131_   ____   ____   ____   ____   ____   ____   ____   ____   ____

   Mode = _____   Median = _____

To find the **mean** of a set of numbers: 2 6 8 3 1 2 6

1 Find the **total** of the numbers: 2 + 6 + 8 + 3 + 1 + 2 + 6 = **28**
2 Count how many numbers are in the set = **7**
3 Divide the total by the number of numbers in the set: **28 ÷ 7 = 4**

The **mean** (or average) is **4**.

3. **Below are the shoe sizes of eight 11-year-olds.**

What is their mean shoe size? _____

3   4   5   3   4   4   2   7

4. **Below are the weights of five 11-year-olds.**

What is their mean weight? _____ kg

45 kg   39 kg   46 kg   42 kg   43 kg

0		6
Tough	OK	Got it!

Total

6

Challenge yourself

Ask someone to choose 21 numbers at random between 1 and 10.
Write them in the box below.

QUICK TIP!
You might need a
calculator to help you
find the mean of the
numbers!

Find the mode, median and mean of the numbers.

Mode = _____   Median = _____   Mean = _____

Fractions

The same fraction can be written in a number of ways.

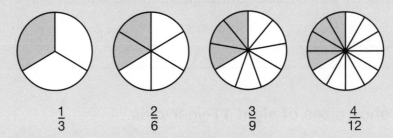

$\frac{1}{3}$ $\frac{2}{6}$ $\frac{3}{9}$ $\frac{4}{12}$

Look carefully at these fractions.

$\frac{1}{3}$ $\frac{2}{6}$ $\frac{3}{9}$ $\frac{4}{12}$ **are all the same size**, or **equivalent** to each other.

They are called **equivalent fractions**.
Notice how the numerator and the denominator are
multiplied by the same number to find an equivalent fraction.

QUICK TIP!

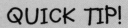

$\frac{1}{3}$ ←— numerator
←— denominator.

1. **Write the equivalent fractions.**

   a $\frac{1}{5}$ $\frac{2}{10}$ _____ _____ _____ _____

   b $\frac{1}{6}$ _____ _____ _____ _____ _____

2. **Complete these addition and subtraction number sentences. Remember to use your knowledge of equivalent fractions.**

   a $\frac{2}{6} + \frac{6}{12} =$ ____   **b** $1\frac{3}{9} + \frac{5}{9} =$ ____   **c** $\frac{7}{10} - \frac{2}{5} =$ ____

   d $\frac{1}{3} - \frac{4}{6} =$ ____   **e** $2\frac{4}{5} + 1\frac{3}{15} =$ ____   **f** $\frac{7}{9} - \frac{8}{18} =$ ____

3. **Order these fractions, smallest first.**

   $\frac{2}{3}$ $\frac{1}{4}$ $\frac{1}{12}$ $\frac{3}{4}$ $\frac{11}{12}$ $\frac{3}{6}$

   _____ _____ _____ _____ _____ _____

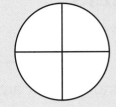
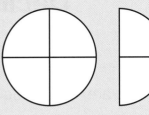

$\frac{14}{4} = 3\frac{1}{2}$

There are 14 quarters in $3\frac{1}{2}$.

QUICK TIP!
An improper fraction has a numerator larger than the denominator

4. **Change these improper fractions into mixed numbers.**

   a $\frac{17}{5} = 3\frac{2}{5}$　　　　b $\frac{16}{3} = 5\overline{3}$　　　　c $\frac{21}{4} =$ ____　　　　d $\frac{46}{9} =$ ____

   e $\frac{30}{7} =$ ____　　　　f $\frac{17}{2} =$ ____　　　　g $\frac{36}{9} =$ ____　　　　h $\frac{25}{8} =$ ____

5. **Write three more fractions that are equivalent to …**

   a $\frac{9}{12}$ ____ ____ ____　　　　b $\frac{2}{7}$ ____ ____ ____

   c $\frac{1}{1}$ ____ ____ ____　　　　d $\frac{11}{10}$ ____ ____ ____

   e $\frac{40}{100}$ ____ ____ ____　　　　f $\frac{24}{48}$ ____ ____ ____

6. **Write the simple fraction for each of these decimal fractions.**

   a $0.75 = \frac{3}{4}$　　　　b $0.9 =$ ____　　　　c $0.25 =$ ____　　　　d $0.333 =$ ____

Tough	OK	Got it!

0　　　　　　　　　　　　　　　　　　　　　　　　　　　　26

Total

$\frac{}{26}$

Challenge yourself

Multiply these fractions.

Example: $\frac{1}{4} \times \frac{1}{2} = \frac{1}{8}$

   a $\frac{1}{4} \times \frac{1}{3} =$ ____　　　　b $\frac{1}{5} \times \frac{1}{2} =$ ____　　　　c $\frac{1}{6} \times \frac{1}{3} =$ ____　　　　d $\frac{1}{4} \times \frac{1}{5} =$ ____

Divide these fractions by these whole numbers.

Example: $\frac{1}{3} \div 2 = \frac{1}{6}$

   e $\frac{1}{4} \div 2 =$ ____　　　　f $\frac{1}{6} \div 2 =$ ____　　　　g $\frac{1}{4} \div 4 =$ ____　　　　h $\frac{1}{3} \div 3 =$ ____

Decimals

Decimals are numbers that are, or include amounts that are, less than 1.

$2 \cdot 3 = 2$ units and 3 tenths $= 2\frac{3}{10}$

0·1 can be split into 10 equal smaller parts called hundredths, like this:

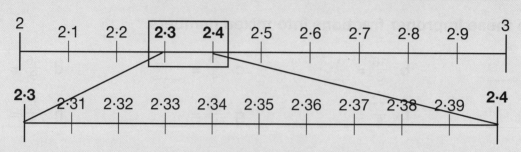

$2 \cdot 36 = 2$ units, 3 tenths and 6 hundredths $= 2\frac{36}{100}$

0·01 can be split into 10 equal smaller parts called thousandths.

$2 \cdot 364 = 2$ units, 3 tenths, 6 hundredths and 4 thousandths $= 2\frac{364}{1\,000}$

1. **Match the written number with the correct card. Join the dots.**

   a Eight units, three tenths and two hundredths   ●   ● 13·19

   b Two units, six tenths and one thousandth   ●   ● 6·054

   c Thirteen units, one tenth and nine hundredths   ●   ● 5·55

   d Six units, five hundredths and four thousandths   ●   ● 2·601

   e Twenty-two units, eight tenths and one hundredth   ●   ● 8·32

   f Five units, five tenths and five hundredths   ●   ● 22·81

2. **Continue these patterns.**

   a

3·26	3·28	3·30	3·32				

   b

4·65	4·70	4·75				5·00

3. **Place these decimals on the number line.**
Use arrows to show where they go.

10·89   10·99   11·16

4. **Round to the nearest whole number.**

a 9·65 _____   9·38 _____   9·55 _____

b 56·89 _____   56·98 _____   56·09 _____

5. **Place these in order, largest first.**

0.375   25% $\frac{1}{8}$ 99%   0.55 $\frac{2}{3}$

_____   _____   _____   _____   _____   _____

0		Tough		OK		Got it!	**12**

Total

12

Challenge yourself

Multiply these numbers.

	× 10	× 100	× 1 000
4·23			
7·06			
16·9			

Divide these numbers.

	÷ 10	÷ 100	÷ 1 000
24·9			
156·12			
774·2			

Coordinates

Coordinates allow us to find an exact place on a grid.
This grid shows clearly the **x-axis** and
y-axis. It is divided into four **quadrants**.

QUICK TIP!
The axes divide the
grid into four sections
called **quadrants**.

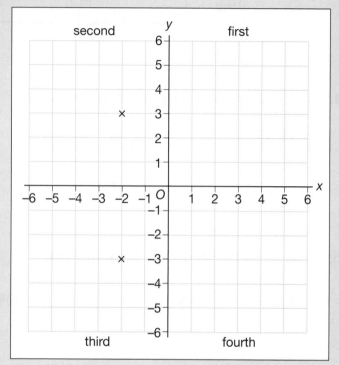

The coordinates of the point marked X in
the second quadrant are (–2, 3).
Remember, you always go **across first**.
If the coordinates are translated into the
third quadrant reflected on the x-axis, the new coordinates would be (–2, –3).

1. **Place neat crosses on this grid for the coordinates listed.**

(–3, 3)
(2, 1)
(–3, –4)
(–5, –2)
(2, –2)
(0, 3)
(–5, 1)
(0, –4)

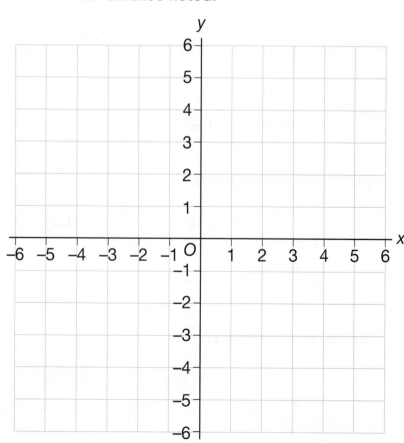

Neatly join the crosses in order.

What shape have you drawn? _____

2. **Write the coordinates of a rectangle using the grid below.**

Each vertex should be in a different quadrant!

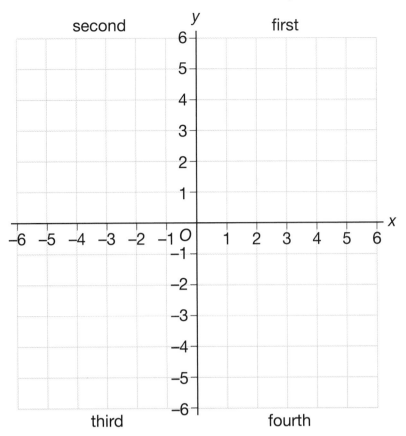

second   first

third   fourth

_____ _____ _____ _____

0   Tough   OK   Got it!   2

Total

2

Challenge yourself

Write the coordinates of the square if it were reflected in the *x*-axis.

a _____ _____

    _____ _____

Write the coordinates of the square if it were reflected in the *y*-axis.

b _____ _____

    _____ _____

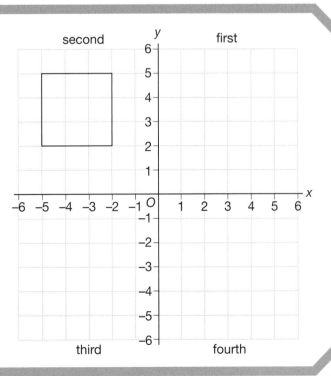

second   first

third   fourth

How am I doing?

1. **Put these numbers in order, smallest first.**

   a   5 644 345   5 654 345   5 566 645   5 664 345

   _____   _____   _____   _____

   b   1 923 647   1 923 547   1 923 748   1 923 648

   _____   _____   _____   _____

2. **Continue the number sequences.**

   a

2·8	4·1	5·4	6·7				

   b

156	139	122	105				

3. **Add or subtract …**

   a   6 2 3 7
       + 1 3 7 8
       _____

   b   1 7 2 6
       + 3 3 9 1
       _____

   c   3 6 9
        − 1 5 3
        _____

   d   7 3 6
        − 2 8 5
        _____

4. **Multiply …**

   a   1 2 5
       ×   1 6

   b   3 3 4
       ×   2 1

   c   1 2 5
       ×   1 6

5. a $7 \times 3 =$ _____   b $8 \times$ _____ $= 56$ c _____ $\times 4 = 24$

   d $7 \times 9 =$ _____   e $5 \times$ _____ $= 25$ f $4 \times$ _____ $= 16$

   g $6 \times$ _____ $= 54$ h _____ $\times 6 = 48$ i $9 \times$ _____ $= 81$

6. **Find the mean of these numbers.**

   a 7 4 5 8 2 4   Mean = _____

   b 2 6 7 12 8   Mean = _____

7. **Write the equivalent fractions.**

   a $\frac{1}{2}$ $\frac{2}{}$ ___   ___   ___   ___

   $\frac{}{8}$

   b $\frac{1}{5}$ ___   ___   ___ $\frac{5}{}$ ___

   $\frac{}{20}$

   c $\frac{1}{3}$ ___   ___   ___   ___   ___

8. **Multiply each of these numbers by 100.**

   a 45·67 _____   **b** 7·823 _____   **c** 215·455 _____

9. **Write the coordinates of the vertices of this square.**

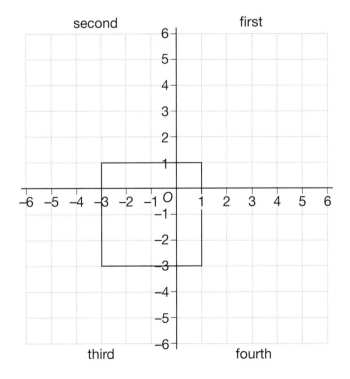

(,) (,)
(,) (,)

Total

29

21

Negative numbers

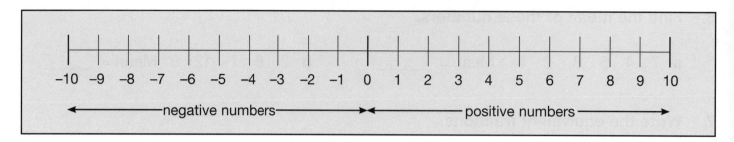

negative numbers ← → positive numbers

1. Put these integers in order, smallest first.

a

7	−8	5	−1	−3	6
−8	−3	−1	5	6	7

> **QUICK TIP!**
> An **integer** is a whole number. It can be more, less or the same as zero.

b

−15	20	33	−18	2	5

c

12	2	−12	0	1	−2

d

−28	−36	−54	−12	−14	−21

e

21	−1	31	−5	−14	16

f

−3	30	33	−300	−303	−30

g

62	21	−14	38	61	−7

2. Solve these problems.

a The temperature is –2 °C. It rises by 6 °C.
What is the temperature now? _____ °C.

b The temperature is –8 °C. It rises by 8 °C.
What is the temperature now? _____ °C.

c The temperature is –5 °C.
How much does it rise to reach 10 °C? _____

d The temperature is –20 °C.
How much does it rise to reach 1 °C? _____

e The temperature is –15 °C. It rises by 7 °C.
What is the temperature now? _____

f The temperature is –6 °C.
How much does it rise to reach 23 °C? _____

0			12
Tough	OK	Got it!	

Total

12 / 12

Challenge yourself

Which integers could ☐ **and** △ **stand for? Make each calculation different.**

a $3 \times \boxed{7} + \triangle_{-4} = 17$

b $3 \times \square + \triangle = 17$

c $3 \times \square + \triangle = 17$

d $3 \times \square + \triangle = 17$

e $3 \times \square + \triangle = 17$

f $3 \times \square + \triangle = 17$

g $3 \times \square + \triangle = 17$

h $3 \times \square + \triangle = 17$

Multiplication involving decimals

When multiplying decimals, it is a good idea to make an approximation of the answer first.

5·2 × 4 = ?   5·2 × 4 is approximately 5 × 4 which equals 20.

So the answer should be close to 20.

$$5·2 × 4 \quad (5.0 × 4) = 20.0$$
$$(0.2 × 4) = \underline{0.8}$$
$$\underline{\mathbf{20.8}}$$

QUICK TIP!
Remember, the decimal points must always line up under each other.

1. **Write the approximate answer to these multiplication number sentences.**

    a 6·1 × 7 = ? $6 × 7 = 42$ **b** 3·9 × 4 = ? _____

    c 2·7 × 8 = ? _____   **d** 5·8 × 2 = ? _____

    e 9·9 × 6 = ? _____   **f** 1·4 × 9 = ? _____

2. **Find the answers.**

    a 4·9 × 4 (___ × ___) = _____   **b** 7·1 × 8 (___ × ___) = _____

    　　　　　(___ × ___) = _____   　　　　　(___ × ___) = _____

    　　　　　　　　___   　　　　　　　　___

    c 3·6 × 2 (___ × ___) = _____   **d** 5·8 × 7 (___ × ___) = _____

    　　　　　(___ × ___) = _____   　　　　　(___ × ___) = _____

    　　　　　　　　___   　　　　　　　　___

    e 1·9 × 9 (___ × ___) = _____   **f** 3·5 × 6 (___ × ___) = _____

    　　　　　(___ × ___) = _____   　　　　　(___ × ___) = _____

    　　　　　　　　___   　　　　　　　　___

3. **Complete these number sentences.**

    a 5·9 × 2 = _____   **b** 6·6 × 6 = _____   **c** 3·4 × 9 = _____

This is how to multiply decimals to two decimal points.

5·23 × 4 = ?   5·23 × 4 is approximately 5 × 4 which equals 20.

Again, the answer should be close to 20.   5·23 × 4   (5·00 × 4) = 20·00
                                                          (0·20 × 4) =   0·80
                                                          (0·03 × 4) =   0·12
                                                                    ────────
                                                                      20·92

4. **Fill the gaps.**

a 3·21 × 4(_____ × _____) = _____   b 6·19 × 5 (_____ × _____) = _____

      (_____ × _____) = _____   (_____ × _____) = _____

      (_____ × _____) = _____   (_____ × _____) = _____

            _____   _____

c 4·67 × 3(_____ × _____) = _____   d 2·18 × 6 (_____ × _____) = _____

      (_____ × _____) = _____   (_____ × _____) = _____

      (_____ × _____) = _____   (_____ × _____) = _____

            _____   _____

0	Tough	OK	Got it! **18**

Total
/18

Challenge yourself

Solve the problems.

£9.75

a Crudwell football team needs to replace five of its football shirts.
   Each new shirt will cost £9.75.
   How much will it cost to replace all five football shirts? _____

b For Annabel's birthday treat she has invited eight friends to visit the zoo.
   It costs £5.30 plus 45p for some food to feed the animals, for each child.
   How much does it cost for Annabel and her friends to visit the zoo and feed
   the animals? _____

Division

Do you remember?
We divide large numbers like this ...

$189 \div 9$	$9 \overline{)189}$
How many 9s in 1? 0 r1	$9 \overline{)1^189}$
How many 9s in 18? 2	$\begin{array}{r} 2 \\ 9 \overline{)1^189} \end{array}$
How many 9s in 9? 1	$\begin{array}{r} 2\ 1 \\ 9 \overline{)189} \end{array}$
$189 \div 9 = 21$	

1. **Divide ...**

a $5 \overline{)255}$ b $7 \overline{)714}$

c $6 \overline{)366}$ d $4 \overline{)648}$

e $3 \overline{)429}$ f $5 \overline{)156}$

g $8 \overline{)249}$ h $7 \overline{)499}$

i $4 \overline{)328}$ j $5 \overline{)359}$

k $6 \overline{)547}$ l $2 \overline{)187}$

m $8 \overline{)248}$ n $9 \overline{)219}$

QUICK TIP!
Watch out! Some of these answers have remainders!

For your workings

Look carefully at this.

This is how we can do long division.

$432 \div 15$ becomes

```
            2   8   r 12
    1 5 | 4 3 2
        -3 0 0   (15 × 20)
          1 3 2
         -1 2 0   (15 × 8)
            1 2
```

2. **Divide …**

| For your workings |

a $36\overline{)725}$

b $21\overline{)847}$

c $46\overline{)929}$

d $28\overline{)843}$

0			18
Tough	OK	Got it!	

Total

/18

Challenge yourself

Solve these problems.

a Five children went carol singing. They collected £62·25 and a handful of sweets! How much money did they each get? _____

b Jess earned £666 in one year doing different jobs for all her neighbours. If the money was divided equally, how much did she earn each month? _____

Calculations

Do you remember which are odd and which are even numbers?

2 4 6 8 10 = **even numbers**
1 3 5 7   9 = **odd numbers**

Here are some quick, simple rules that will help you check the possibility of your answers being right.

- **The sum of two even numbers is even:**
  3 612 + 5 876 = answer will be an even number

- **The sum of two odd numbers is even:**
  6 577 + 2 183 = answer will be an even number

- **The sum of one odd and one even number is odd:**
  3 657 + 2 186 = answer will be an odd number

> **QUICK TIP!**
> Knowing these rules helps you check whether an answer is reasonable or not!

1. **Write whether these answers will be odd or even.**

    a 218 + 567 = _odd_

    b 369 + 217 = _____

    c 1 856 + 3 962 = _____

    d 3 691 + 1 285 = _____

    e 9 999 + 111 = _____

    f 317 + 5 896 = _____

    g 7 963 + 7 962 = _____

> **QUICK TIP!**
> Again, knowing this can help you check whether an answer is reasonable.

Remember ... there are ways of checking addition, subtraction, multiplication and division number sentences by changing them round.

Look at these.
587 + 623 = 1 210 $\longrightarrow$ 1 210 − 623 = 587
381 × 19 = 7 239 $\longrightarrow$ 7 239 ÷ 381 = 19

2. **Look at the second column.**

Put a ✓ if the number sentences are correct or a ✗ if they are wrong.

a $217 + 5698 = 5915$ $5915 - 216 = 5698$ ☐

b $27 \times 35 = 945$ $945 \div 27 = 35$ ☐

c $1035 \div 23 = 45$ $45 \times 24 = 1035$ ☐

d $567 - 278 = 289$ $277 + 289 = 567$ ☐

e $1289 + 3698 = 4987$ $4987 - 1289 = 3698$ ☐

f $1032 \div 12 = 86$ $86 \times 12 = 1031$ ☐

g $7891 - 397 = 7494$ $7594 + 7891 = 387$ ☐

h $23 \times 23 = 529$ $529 \div 23 = 24$ ☐

i $7750 \div 125 = 62$ $125 \times 62 = 7750$ ☐

Tough	OK	Got it!

0 15

Total

15

Challenge yourself

The BODMAS rule

When you do a calculation that has two or more parts and includes multiplication and division you must do the operations in a specific order. BODMAS tells us that order.

B = brackets ( )
O = other powers e.g. ^{2}
D = division ÷
M = multiplication ×
A = addition +
S = subtraction −

Do these calculations using the BODMAS rule.

a $15 + 23 \times 2 =$ _____

b $50 - 15 \div 3 \times 9 =$ _____

c $3 \times (29 - 13) =$ _____

d $5^2 + (20 \times 4) =$ _____

Percentages

Remember, **percentages** are a way of dividing whole numbers into hundredths.

A percentage is the number of parts in every 100.

per cent = in every 100

1 per cent = 1 in every 100

50 per cent = 50 in every 100

1 per cent can be written as $\frac{1}{100}$ or **0.01** or **1%**

50 per cent can be written as $\frac{50}{100}$ or **0.5** or **50%**

QUICK TIP!
Remember, the sign for per cent is **%**.

1. **Percentages, fractions and decimals are different ways of writing the same amount. Complete this table.**

Fractions	Decimals	Percentages
		1%
	0·02	
$\frac{17}{100}$		
$\frac{1}{5}$		
		25%
	0·35	
$\frac{1}{2}$		
$\frac{6}{10}$		
	0·75	
		100%

Sometimes we need to find the percentage of whole numbers.

What is 10% of 40?
This means we need to find $\frac{1}{10}$ of 40.
We divide 40 by 10 = 4
This means 10% of 40 = 4

Now, what is 20% of 40?
This means we need to find $\frac{2}{10}$ of 40.
We know 10% of 40 = 4
So ... 20% of 40 = 2 lots of 10%
= 2 × 4
= 8

2. **Find the percentages of these whole numbers.**

a 10% of 20 = _____   20% of 20 = _____

b 10% of 50 = _____   20% of 50 = _____

c 10% of 120 = _____   20% of 120 = _____

d 10% of 240 = _____   20% of 240 = _____

3. **Now try these.**

a 30% of 50 = _____   **b** 70% of 100 = _____

c 50% of 26 = _____   **d** 40% of 40 = _____

e 15% of 40 = _____   **f** 25% of 80 = _____

g 25% of 200 = _____   **h** 15% of 60 = _____

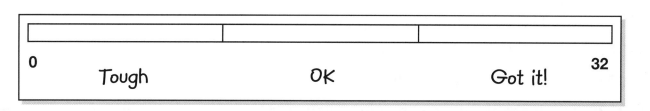

			Total
0			
Tough	OK	Got it! **32**	**32**

Challenge yourself

Answer these questions.

A shop is selling all of its DVDs with a 20% discount.

a If the full price of a DVD is £10·00 how much would it be with 20% off?   _____

b If the full price of a DVD is £8·00 how much would it be with 20% off?   _____

c If the full price of a DVD is £15·00 how much would it be with 20% off?   _____

Rounding numbers

When we round a number we round it to a nearby value.

Remember …

If the digit is 4 or less we round **down**.	34 is rounded down to 30
If the digit is 5 or more we round **up**.	35 is rounded up to 40

If we are rounding to the **nearest 10** we look at the digit in the **units** column.

72 rounded to the nearest 10 is 70

If we are rounding to the **nearest 100** we look at the digit in the **tens** column.

172 rounded to the nearest 100 is 200

If we are rounding to the **nearest 1 000** we look at the digit in the **hundreds** column and so on.

1 172 rounded to the nearest 1 000 is 1 000

1. **Fill in the gaps in the following sentences.**

   a **45 378** rounded to the nearest hundred is _____.

   45 378 rounded to the nearest ten thousand is _____.

   b **8 686 868** rounded to the nearest ten thousand is _____.

   8 686 868 rounded to the nearest million is _____.

   c **58 737** rounded to the nearest ten thousand is _____.

   58 737 rounded to the nearest thousand is _____.

   d **3 459 332** rounded to the nearest thousand is _____.

   3 459 332 rounded to the nearest hundred thousand is _____.

   e **864 644** rounded to the nearest thousand is _____.

   864 644 rounded to the nearest ten thousand is _____.

   f **9 919 959** rounded to the nearest ten thousand is _____.

   9 919 959 rounded to the nearest ten is _____.

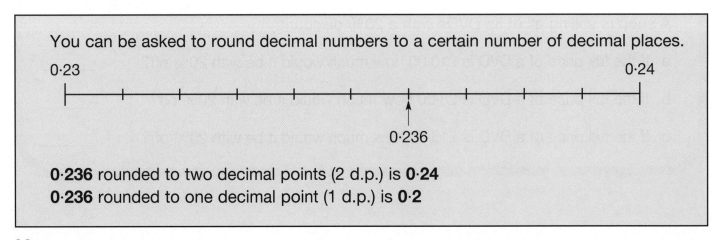

You can be asked to round decimal numbers to a certain number of decimal places.

0·23   0·24

0·236

0·236 rounded to two decimal points (2 d.p.) is **0·24**
0·236 rounded to one decimal point (1 d.p.) is **0·2**

Bond

No Nonsense
Maths

10–11 years

Parents' notes

What your child will learn from this book

Bond No Nonsense will help your child to understand and become more confident in their maths work. This book features all the main maths objectives covered by your child's class teacher during the school year. It provides clear, straightforward teaching and learning of the essentials in a rigorous, step-by-step way.

How you can help

Following a few simple guidelines will ensure that your child gets the best from this book:

- Explain that the book will help your child become confident in their maths work.
- If your child has difficulty reading the text on the page or understanding a question, do provide help.
- Provide scrap paper to give your child extra space for rough working.
- Encourage your child to complete all the exercises in a lesson. You can mark the work using this answer section. Your child can record their own impressions of the work using the 'How did I do?' feature.

0			19
	Tough	OK	Got it!

- The 'How am I doing?' sections provide a further review of progress.

Bond No Nonsense 10–11 years Answers

① Numbers and place value pp2–3

1 a 6038002 **b** 9100055 **c** 3577011
d 5801360 **e** 9999909
2 a 70000 **b** 8000 **c** 3000000
d 90000 **e** 100
3 a four million, three hundred and twenty-three thousand, six hundred and seventy-five
b three hundred and eight thousand and four
c seven million, four thousand, three hundred and ninety-nine
4 a 1000000 110011 100100 100001 11011
b 3617423 3167243 2736541 2634751 2367451
c 6655442 5566442 5544662 4466552 4455662
5 a 56438 > 56348 **b** 156839 < 165893
c 33765 > 33675 **d** 58375 < 58377
e 9867563 < 9876562 **f** 776777 > 776677
6 a 1000 **b** 1 **c** 200 **d** 200000

Challenge yourself
Answers will vary

② Number sequences and properties pp4–5

1 a the numbers decrease 13 at a time
b the numbers decrease 25 at a time
c the numbers decrease 0·25 at a time
2 a 90, 112, 134, 156, 178 **b** 375, 352, 329, 306, 283
c 39, 23, 7, –9, –25 **d** 271, 280, 289, 298, 307
3 a 3, 5 **b** 2, 4 **c** 3, 5, 9 **d** 2, 5, 10 **e** 2, 3, 4, 6, 7
f 3 **g** 2, 4 **h** 2, 3, 4, 6, 11, 12 **i** 5
j 2, 3, 4, 6, 8, 9
4 The last two digits would have to be 00, 25, 50 or 75.

Challenge yourself
a 8, 13, 21, 34, 55; Add together the last two numbers
b 32, 64, 128, 256, 512; Double the last number
c 122, 365, 1094, 3281, 9842; Multiply the last number by 3 and take away 1 (or equivalent)

③ Addition and subtraction pp6–7

1 a 12540 **b** 9599 **c** 4689 **d** 3889 **e** 5873
f 68 **g** 8810 **h** 8777 **i** 845
2 a 4857 **b** £145
c Yes, there is 42p left. **d** 1289 seats, 2176 seats

Challenge yourself
a 99762 **b** 26799 **c** 126561 **d** 72963

④ Short and long multiplication pp8–9

1 a 112 **b** 390 **c** 192 **d** 1897 **e** 978 **f** 1547

2 a
```
    422
 ×   23
  8440 (422 × 20)
  1266 (422 × 3)
  9706
```
b
```
    521
 ×   27
 10420 (521 × 20)
  3647 (521 × 7)
 14067
```
c
```
    151
 ×   31
  4530 (151 × 30)
   151 (151 × 1)
  4681
```
d
```
    202
 ×   34
  6060 (202 × 30)
   808 (202 × 4)
  6868
```
e
```
   1235
 ×   41
 49400 (1235 × 40)
  1235 (1235 × 1)
 50635
```
f
```
   2351
 ×   51
 17550 (2351 × 50)
  2351 (2351 × 1)
 119901
```

Challenge yourself
a 6110 **b** £13·44 **c** 3375

⑤ Times tables pp10–11

1 18 49 56 16 18 54 36 42 21 9 45 40 80 54 24
40 27 64 48 0 35 14 81 25 24 28 4 100 50 1 12 30
60 32 44 21 81 7 108 10 121 24 48 27 70 15 77 144

2 a 45 **b** 64 **c** 21 **d** 32 **e** 63 **f** 36 **g** 60 **h** 40
i 56 **j** 18 **k** 16 **l** 96
3 a 5 **b** 9 **c** 2 **d** 8 **e** 7 **f** 8 **g** 10 **h** 8
i 8 **j** 3 **k** 9 **l** 10

Challenge yourself
Answers will vary but include
a 4 × 6 = 24 **b** 6 × 9 = 54 **c** 6 × 8 = 48 **d** 7 × 7 = 49
e 1 × 2 = 2 **f** 9 × 8 = 72 **g** 6 × 6 = 36 **h** 2 × 9 = 18
i 3 × 3 = 9 **j** 7 × 9 = 63

⑥ Mode, median and mean pp12–13

1 a Mode = 3, Median = 5
b 1 1 1 2 3 4 6 6 7 Mode = 1, Median = 3
c 2 2 2 3 5 5 6 7 9 Mode = 2, Median = 5
2 129 131 131 131 132 133 136 136 137 138 139
Mode = 131, Median = 133
3 4 **4** 43 kg

Challenge yourself
Answers will vary

⑦ Fractions pp14–15

1 a $\frac{2}{10}$ $\frac{3}{15}$ $\frac{4}{20}$ $\frac{5}{25}$ $\frac{6}{30}$ **b** $\frac{2}{12}$ $\frac{3}{18}$ $\frac{4}{24}$ $\frac{5}{30}$ $\frac{6}{36}$

2 a $\frac{10}{12}$ or $\frac{5}{6}$ **b** $1\frac{8}{9}$ **c** $\frac{3}{10}$ **d** $\frac{1}{3}$ **e** 4 **f** $\frac{3}{9}$ or $\frac{1}{3}$

3 $\frac{1}{12}$ $\frac{1}{4}$ $\frac{3}{6}$ $\frac{2}{3}$ $\frac{3}{4}$ $\frac{11}{12}$

4 b $5\frac{1}{3}$ **c** $5\frac{1}{4}$ **d** $5\frac{1}{9}$ **e** $4\frac{2}{7}$ **f** $8\frac{1}{2}$ **g** 4 **h** $3\frac{1}{8}$

5 Answers could include:
a $\frac{3}{4}$ $\frac{6}{8}$ $\frac{12}{16}$ **b** $\frac{4}{14}$ $\frac{6}{21}$ $\frac{8}{28}$ **c** $\frac{2}{2}$ $\frac{3}{3}$ $\frac{4}{4}$
d $\frac{22}{20}$ $\frac{33}{30}$ $\frac{44}{40}$ **e** $\frac{4}{10}$ $\frac{2}{5}$ $\frac{20}{50}$ **f** $\frac{1}{2}$ $\frac{2}{4}$ $\frac{12}{24}$

6 b $\frac{9}{10}$ **c** $\frac{1}{4}$ **d** $\frac{1}{3}$

Challenge yourself
a $\frac{1}{12}$ **b** $\frac{1}{10}$ **c** $\frac{1}{18}$ **d** $\frac{1}{20}$ **e** $\frac{1}{8}$ **f** $\frac{1}{12}$ **g** $\frac{1}{16}$ **h** $\frac{1}{9}$

⑧ Decimals pp16–17

1 a 8·32 **b** 2·601 **c** 13·19 **d** 6·054 **e** 22·81 **f** 5·55
2 a 3·34, 3·36, 3·38, 3·40 **b** 4·80, 4·85, 4·90, 4·95
3
```
 |10.89      |10.99              |11.16
 |10·9       |11·0       11·1    |11·2
 +--+--+--+--+--+--+--+--+--+--+--+
```
4 a 10 9 10 **b** 57 57 56
5 99% $\frac{2}{3}$ 0·55 0·375 25% $\frac{1}{8}$

Challenge yourself
× 10 = 42·3 70·6 169
× 100 = 423 706 1690
× 1000 = 4230 7060 16900
÷ 10 = 2·49 15·612 77·42
÷ 100 = 0·249 1·5612 7·742
÷ 1000 = 0·0249 0·15612 0·7742

⑨ Coordinates pp18–19

1 octagon

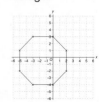

2 Answers will vary

Challenge yourself
a (−5, −2), (−2, −2), (−5, −5), (−2, −5)
b (2, 5), (5, 5), (2, 2), (5, 2)

How am I doing? pp20–21
1 **a** 5 566 645, 5 644 345, 5 654 345, 5 664 345
   b 1 923 547, 1 923 647, 1 923 648, 1 923 748
2 **a** 8·0, 9·3, 10·6, 11·9   **b** 88, 71, 54, 37
3 **a** 7615   **b** 5117   **c** 216   **d** 451
4 **a** 2000   **b** 7014   **c** 2000
5 **a** 21 **b** 7 **c** 6 **d** 63 **e** 5 **f** 4 **g** 9 **h** 8 **i** 9
6 **a** 5   **b** 7
7 **a** $\frac{2}{4}\,\frac{3}{6}\,\frac{4}{8}\,\frac{5}{10}\,\frac{6}{12}$ **b** $\frac{2}{10}\,\frac{3}{15}\,\frac{4}{20}\,\frac{5}{25}\,\frac{6}{30}$ **c** $\frac{2}{6}\,\frac{3}{9}\,\frac{4}{12}\,\frac{5}{15}\,\frac{6}{18}$
8 **a** 4567   **b** 782·3   **c** 21 545·5
9 (1, −3), (1, 1), (−3, −3), (1, 1)

⑩ Negative numbers pp22–23
1 **b** −18, −15, 2, 5, 20, 33   **c** −12, −2, 0, 1, 2, 12
   d −54, −36, −28, −21, −14, −12   **e** −14, −5, −1, 16, 21, 31
   f −303, −300, −30, −3, 30, 33   **g** −14, −7, 21, 38, 61, 62
2 **a** 4°C **b** 0°C **c** 15°C **d** 21°C **e** −8°C **f** 29°C
Challenge yourself
Answers will vary

⑪ Multiplication involving decimals pp24–25
1 **b** 4 × 4 = 16   **c** 3 × 8 = 24   **d** 6 × 2 = 12
   e 10 × 6 = 60   **f** 1 × 9 = 9
2 **a** 4·0 × 4 = 16·0, 0·9 × 4 = 3·6, 19·6
   b 7·0 × 8 = 56·0, 0·1 × 8 = 0·8, 56·8
   c 3·0 × 2 = 6·0, 0·6 × 2 = 1·2, 7·2
   d 5·0 × 7 = 35·0, 0·8 × 7 = 5·6, 40·6
   e 1·0 × 9 = 9·0, 0·9 × 9 = 8·1, 17·1
   f 3·0 × 6 = 18·0, 0·5 × 6 = 3·0, 21·0
3 **a** 11·8   **b** 39·6   **c** 30·6
4 **a** 3·00 × 4 = 12·00, 0·20 × 4 = 0·80, 0·01 × 4 = 0·04, 12·84
   b 6·00 × 5 = 30·00, 0·10 × 5 = 0·50, 0·09 × 5 = 0·45, 30·95
   c 4·00 × 3 = 12·00, 0·60 × 3 = 1·80, 0·07 × 3 = 0·21, 14·01
   d 2·00 × 6 = 12·00, 0·10 × 6 = 0·60, 0·08 × 6 = 0·48, 13·08
Challenge yourself
a £48·75   **b** £51·75

⑫ Division pp26–27
1 **a** 51 **b** 102 **c** 61 **d** 162 **e** 143 **f** 31 r1
   g 31 r1 **h** 71 r2 **i** 82 **j** 71 r4 **k** 91 r1 **l** 93 r1
   m 31 **n** 24 r3
2 **a** 20 r5 **b** 40 r7 **c** 20 r9 **d** 30 r3
Challenge yourself
a £12·45   **b** £55·50

⑬ Calculations pp28–29
1 **b** even **c** even **d** even **e** even **f** odd **g** odd
2 **a** ✗ **b** ✓ **c** ✗ **d** ✗ **e** ✓ **f** ✗ **g** ✗ **h** ✗ **i** ✓
Challenge yourself
a 61   **b** 5   **c** 48   **d** 105

⑭ Percentages p30–31
1

Fractions	Decimals	Percentages
$\frac{1}{100}$	0·01	1%
$\frac{2}{100}$	0·02	2%
$\frac{17}{100}$	0·17	17%
$\frac{1}{5}$	0·2	20%
$\frac{1}{4}$	0·25	25%
$\frac{35}{100}$	0·35	35%
$\frac{1}{2}$	0·5	50%
$\frac{6}{10}$	0·6	60%
$\frac{3}{4}$	0·75	75%
1	1·0	100%

2 **a** 2 4 **b** 5 10 **c** 12 24 **d** 24 48
3 **a** 15 **b** 70 **c** 13 **d** 16 **e** 6 **f** 20 **g** 50 **h** 9
Challenge yourself
a £8.00   **b** £6.40   **c** £12.00

⑮ Rounding numbers pp32–33
1 **a** 45 400, 50 000   **b** 8 690 000, 9 000 000
   c 60 000, 59 000   **d** 3 459 000, 3 500 000
   e 865 000, 860 000   **f** 9 920 000, 9 919 960
2 **a** 0·47 **b** 0·38 **c** 0·72 **d** 0·13
   e 0·88 **f** 0·66 **g** 3·39 **h** 9·11
   i 5·63 **j** 4·49 **k** 7·23 **l** 2·57
3 **a** 0·5 **b** 0·76 **c** 0·899 **d** 5·3
   e 2·79 **f** 0·997 **g** 5·91 **h** 2·889
   i 3·01 **j** 2·6
Challenge yourself
Answers will vary

⑯ Measurements pp34–35
1 **a** mm **b** g **c** m **d** l **e** g **f** cm
2 **a** 1 500 g **b** 1 000 mm **c** 0·3 litres **d** 0·125 kg
   e 2 250 m **f** 50 ml
3 **a** 1·65 m or 165 cm **b** 260 g **c** 171 156 m
4 **a** 40 miles **b** 9 miles **c** 25 miles
Challenge yourself
250 g flour   570 ml milk   2 eggs

⑰ Solving problems pp36–37
1 e.g. **a** 26 ÷ 15   **b** 28 × 43
2 the money is in the biscuit tin
Challenge yourself
Answers will vary

⑱ Line graphs pp38–39
1

Najib's height
2 **a** 115 cm **b** 155 cm **c** 15 cm **d** 15 cm
   e 1–3 yrs or 2–4 yrs **f** 6–10 yrs **g** 100 cm or 1 m
Challenge yourself

How am I doing? pp40–41
1 **a** 14°C **b** 14°C **c** 28°C
2 **a** 53·6 **b** 17·1
3 **a** 41 r2 **b** 24
4 **a** even **b** even **c** odd **d** even
5 **a** 50% **b** 10% **c** 100% **d** 23% **e** 70% **f** 20%
6 **a** 567·98 **b** 0·79 **c** 4·33 **d** 67·68 **e** 33·93 **f** 1·97
7 **a** millilitres **b** metres **c** grams **d** centimetres

⑲ Algebra pp42–43
1 **a** 72 **b** 19 **c** 41 **d** 6 **e** 52
   f 16 **g** 15 **h** 99 **i** 42
2 **a** $a = 2$ **b** $b = 3$ **c** $m = 6$ **d** $c = 7$ **e** $t = 10$ **f** $b = 2$
3 **a** nth term = 3n **b** nth term = 5n **c** nth term = 7n
   d nth term = 10n **e** nth term = 4n
4 **a** 140 **b** 176 **c** 194 **d** 75
Challenge yourself
a $2n + 1$ **b** $4n + 3$

⑳ Square, cube and triangular numbers pp44–45
1 **b** 64 **c** 5^2, 25 **d** 2^2, 4 **e** 9^2, 81 **f** 12^2, 144
   g 7 × 7, 49 **h** 11 × 11, 121
2

1	4	9	16	**25**	**36**	49	**64**	**81**	100	**121**	**144**

3 **a** 4^3, 64 **b** 2^3, 8 **c** 6^3, 216
d 9^3, 729 **e** 5^3, 125 **f** 7^3, 343

4 **b** 1, 8, 27, 64, **125, 216**, 343, **512, 729, 1 000**

5 | 1 | | 3 | | 6 | | **10** | **15** | **21** | **28** |

6 The sequence of triangular numbers is built up by 1 (+2), 3 (+3), 6 (+4) 10 (+5) and so on.

Challenge yourself

| 169 | /45/ | /120/ | 225 |

㉑ Factors, multiples and prime numbers pp46–47

1 **a** 2 5 10 **b** 4 5 10 **c** 9 2 18 **d** 1 2 31 **e** 9 3 27 6
2 **a** 36 78 60 **b** 81 117 36 **c** 60 144 84 **d** 49 28 105
e 15 215 90
3 Coloured numbers: 2, 3, 5, 7, 11, 13, 17, 19, 23, 29, 31, 37, 41, 43, 47, 53, 59, 61, 67, 71, 73, 79, 83, 89, 97

Challenge yourself
a coloured **b** 24th

㉒ Estimation pp48–49

1 **a** 3000 **b** 85 **c** 550 **d** 8000 (approx.)

2 **a** [0 ————————↓———— 1 000] 650 (approx.)
b [0 ——↓———————— 10 000] 2 800 (approx.)
c [−100 ————————↓———— 0] −25 (approx.)

3 **a** 50 (approx.) **b, c, d** Answers will vary

Challenge yourself
Spending one week on holiday, spending ten days in Spain and spending a fortnight skiing are all possible in the time given. Children may refer to having worked out how many days 1 300 000 seconds are equivalent to (15 days).

㉓ Ratio and proportion pp50–51

1 **b** 1:1 1 to every 1 **c** 2:3 2 to every 3 **d** 1:2 1 to every 2
e 3:2 3 to every 2 **f** 2:2 or 1:1 2 to every 2 (or 1 to every 1)
2 **b** $\frac{1}{2}$ **c** $\frac{2}{5}$ **d** $\frac{1}{3}$ **e** $\frac{3}{5}$ **f** $\frac{2}{4}$ or $\frac{1}{2}$
3 **a** 12 girls **b** 6 cakes **c** 16 fish **d** 2 hours 20 minutes

Challenge yourself
The ratio of shape a to shape b is 3:1. The proportion of b's squares to the the total number is $\frac{1}{4}$.

㉔ Area and perimeter p52–53

1 **a** P = 28 cm A = 45 cm² **b** P = 40 cm A = 82 cm²
c P = 30 cm A = 42 cm²
2 **a** r = 50 cm² t = 25 cm² **b** r = 28 cm² t = 14 cm²
c r = 40 cm² t = 20 cm²
3 **a** 45 cm² **b** 42 cm² **c** 24 cm²

Challenge yourself
50 cm, 28 cm, 22 cm, 20 cm
5 different perimeters

㉕ Angles pp54–55

1 **a** b = 45° **b** c = 280° **c** b = 57° **d** b = 108°
e c = 245° **f** b = 88°
2 **a** a = 105° **b** a = 80° **c** a = 62°

Challenge yourself

a
60°
60° 60°
Not to scale

b
100° 80°
80° 100°

㉖ Shapes pp56–57

1 **a** ▭ **b** Example: ✛ **c** ▱

2 **a** cylinder **b** cube **c** triangular prism

A4

3

circumference
diameter radius

4 **a** kite **b** parallelogram **c** scalene triangle **d** trapezium
Challenge yourself
Answers will vary

㉗ Volume pp58–59

1 **a** 24 cm³ **b** 15 cm³ **c** 32 cm³
d 50 cm³ **e** 27 cm³ **f** 60 cm³
2 **a** 80 cm³ **b** 96 cm³ **c** 36 cm³
d 125 cm³ **e** 84 cm³ **f** 72 cm³

Challenge yourself
a 3 cm **b** 6 cm **c** 8 cm

㉘ Probability pp60–61

1 **b** certain **c** unlikely, possible **d** possible **e** impossible
f answers will vary **g** answers will vary
2 Answers will vary
3 Answers will vary

Challenge yourself
a $\frac{1}{6}$ **b** $\frac{1}{6}$ **c** $\frac{1}{6}$ **d** $\frac{1}{6}$

How am I doing? pp62–63

1 **a** 119 **b** 33
2 Answers will vary but could include:
square numbers 25, 36, 49, 64, 81
triangular numbers 21, 28, 36, 45, 55
3 **a** 5, 3 **b** 15, 3, 5, 2, 6, 10 **c** 2, 7, 42, 12
4 **a** [0 ————↓———————— 100] 28 (approx.)
b [0 ——————————↓—— 1 000] 650 (approx.)
c [0 ————↓———————— 10 000] 2 800 (approx.)
5 ratio = 3:4
proportion = $\frac{3}{7}$ black, $\frac{4}{7}$ white
6 P = 36 cm A = 68 cm² **7** **a** 115° **b** 70°
8
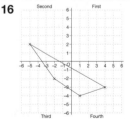
circumference
diameter radius
9 Answers will vary

10–11 years assessment pp64–65

1 220·8
2 A prime number is only divisible by itself and 1.
Answers will vary but include: 3, 5, 7, 11, 13, 17
3 **a** 100% **b** 50%
4 Mode = 6 Median = 6
5 15 °C **6** 22 **7** No **8** 29 **9** 28·8 **10** Yes
11 $6\frac{2}{8}$ or $6\frac{1}{4}$ **12** 2·87, 2·78, 2·287, 2·278, 0·278
13 **a** 8·9 **b** 12·8 **c** 333·3
14 12 376 **15** 23rd term = 138
16
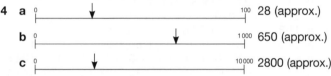

17 Answers will vary **18** 8 **19** Answers will vary **20** 24
21 **a** triangle **b** acute **c** quadrilateral
22 A = 37 cm² P = 26 cm
23

24 Answers will vary **25** Volume = length × width × height

2. Round these numbers to two decimal places.

a 0·468 _____

b 0·378 _____

c 0·723 _____

d 0·127 _____

e 0·881 _____

f 0·659 _____

g 3·387 _____

h 9·111 _____

i 5·632 _____

j 4·487 _____

k 7·225 _____

l 2·566 _____

3. Round these numbers to the given decimal place.

a 0·453 to 1 d.p. = _____

b 0·763 to 2 d.p. = _____

c 0·8989 to 3 d.p. = _____

d 5·34 to 1 d.p. = _____

e 2·785 to 2 d.p. = _____

f 0·9972 to 3 d.p. = _____

g 5·9136 to 1 d.p. = _____

h 2·8888 to 3 d.p. = _____

i 3·008 to 2 d.p. = _____

j 2·555 to 1 d.p. = _____

0		28
Tough	OK	Got it!

Total

28

Challenge yourself

Round the numbers in these number sentences so that you are able to make a sensible estimate of the answer.

a 4576 + 23799 = 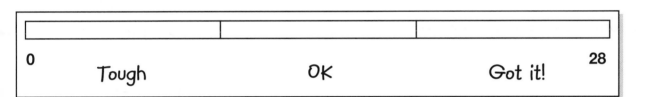 4600 + 23800 = 28400

b 8927 + 7739 = _____ = _____

c 34·7 − 17·2 = _____ = _____

d 518 × 22 = _____ = _____

e 6099 − 5498 = _____ = _____

f 348976 + 278889 = _____ = _____

Measurements

Standard metric units of measure for ...

Length	Mass	Capacity
millimetre (**mm**)	gram (**g**)	millilitre (**ml**)
centimetre (**cm**)	kilogram (**kg**)	centilitre (**cl**)
metre (**m**)	tonne	litre (**l**)
kilometre (**km**)		

1. **Which unit of measure would you use to measure ...**

   a the thickness of a rubber band? _____

   b the weight of an insect? _____

   c the depth of a swimming pool? _____

   d the contents of a bottle of lemonade? _____

   e the weight of a bag of crisps? _____

   f the width of a door? _____

2. **Convert these measurements.**

   a 1·5 kg = _____ g

   b 1 m = _____ mm

   c 300 ml = _____ l

   d 125 g = _____ kg

   e 2·25 km = _____ m

   f 0·05 l = _____ ml

3. **Solve these problems.**

   a A group of friends made a daisy chain of 2·5 m. When they were holding it up to show their teacher, 85 cm broke away.

   What length of the daisy chain was left? _____

b How many grams of sugar need to be added to 1·24 kg to make 1·5 kg altogether?

_____

c In an endurance competition, the first glider travelled 16·28 km, the second travelled 153·32 km and the third 1 556 m.

How many metres did the three gliders travel altogether? _____

4. **This sign shows distances in kilometres. Using the conversion graph, rewrite the sign in miles.**

London	65 km
Reading	15 km
Oxford	40 km

a London _____ miles

b Reading _____ miles

c Oxford _____ miles

Tough	OK	Got it!

0   18

Total

____ / 18

Challenge yourself

Change this pancake recipe to approximate metric units.

Pancakes
~
9 oz flour

1 pint of milk

2 eggs

Pancakes
~
_____ **g flour**

_____ **ml of milk**

_____ **eggs**

Solving problems

Solving problems in maths is a way of playing with numbers.
Approach each problem as a challenge!

Calculators can help to speed up the process of finding the answer.

1. **Use a calculator to help you solve these problems.**

   a The answer is 1·7333333.
   Using two 2-digit whole numbers and a ÷ sign, write the number sentence with this answer.

   _____

For your workings

   b The answer is 1 204.
   Using two 2-digit whole numbers and a × sign, write the number sentence with this answer.

   _____

For your workings

2. **You are a detective.**

You have been asked to crack the following code as quickly as possible to find the money!

You know each letter of the alphabet is a number between 1 and 9. The letters of the alphabet are numbered in order 1 to 9 and then repeated 1 to 9 until the alphabet is complete.

Crack the code.

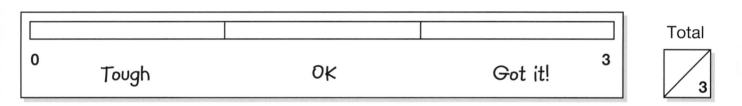

285   46557   91   95   285   2913392   295

0 Tough	OK	Got it! 3

Total

/3

Challenge yourself

Write a 'real life' number story for each of these calculations.

a   25·95 × 15 = 389·25

_____

_____

b   19·23 − 2·89 = 16·34

_____

_____

Line graphs

Line graphs are used for continuous data, like the growth of a plant over three weeks or the changes in temperature over a month.

Lines join the points, clearly showing the changes made, usually over time.

1. **Draw a line graph to show the following data.**

Najib's height

age	1 yr	2 yrs	3 yrs	4 yrs	5 yrs	6 yrs	7 yrs	8 yrs	9 yrs	10 yrs	11 yrs
height	65 cm	80 cm	100 cm	115 cm	125 cm	135 cm	140 cm	145 cm	150 cm	155 cm	165 cm

Remember to:
* include three titles, one for each axis and one to explain the whole graph
* decide what interval the height axis should increase by
* join the dots neatly.

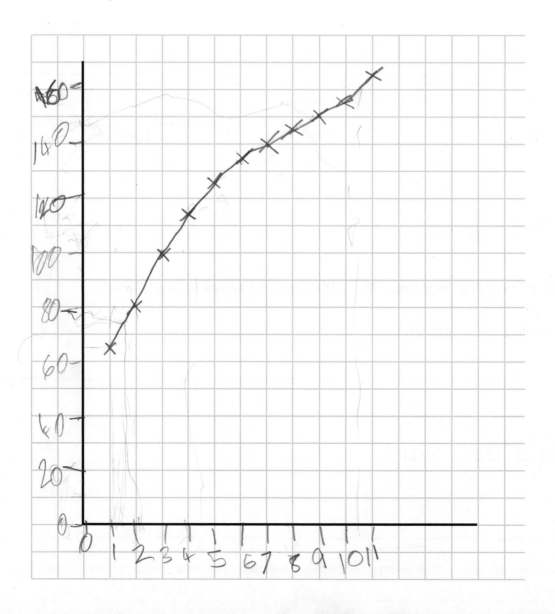

2. **Look carefully at the graph you have drawn. Now answer these questions.**

a   What was Najib's height when he was 4?   _____

b   What was Najib's height when he was 10?   _____

c   Between the ages of 6 and 9 how much did Najib grow?   _____

d   Between the ages of 9 and 11 how much did Najib grow?   _____

e   In which 2-year period did Najib grow the fastest?   _____

f   Between which birthdays was Najib's growth constantly 5 cm a year?   _____

g   What is the increase in Najib's height between the years 1 and 11?   _____

Tough	OK	Got it!

0   8

Total

⬜ 8

Challenge yourself

Draw the information in this table into the pie chart.

Number of children	Favourite potato type
5	roast
10	chips
1	jacket
4	mash

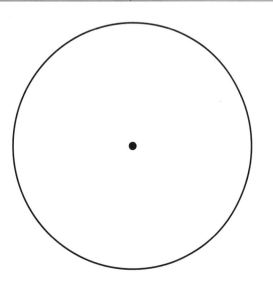

39

How am I doing?

1. **a** The temperature is –8 °C. How much must it rise to reach 6 °C? _____

   b The temperature is 11 °C. How much must it drop to reach –3 °C? _____

   c The temperature is –14 °C. How much must it rise to reach 14 °C? _____

2. **Calculate the answers.**

   a $6.7 \times 8 =$ _____

   b $3.42 \times 5 =$ _____

For your workings

3. **Calculate the answers.**

   a $248 \div 6 =$ _____

   b $312 \div 13 =$ _____

For your workings

4. **Will the answers be odd or even?**

   a $369 + 217 =$ _____   **b** $892 + 586 =$ _____

   c $674 + 233 =$ _____   **d** $567 + 341 =$ _____

5. **Fill in the missing percentages.**

a $\frac{1}{2}$ = _____ %

b 0·1 = _____ %

c 1 = _____ %

d $\frac{23}{100}$ = _____ %

e 0·7 = _____ %

f $\frac{1}{5}$ = _____ %

6. **Round these numbers to two decimal places.**

a 567·981 _____

b 0·7872 _____

c 4·333 _____

d 67·676 _____

e 33·929 _____

f 1·9695 _____

7. **Join the dots to indicate which unit of measure you would use to measure ...**

a the contents of a mug ●   ● grams

b the height of a tree ●   ● metres

c the weight of 10 peas ●   ● centimetres

d the width of a calculator ●   ● millilitres

Total

27

Algebra

Algebra is the use of symbols in describing mathematical patterns.

There are some tips to remember when writing algebra.
(Any letters can be used, here we have used the letters $a = 6$ and $b = 3$)

a = represents an individual number $\quad a = 6$

$ab = a \times b$ $\qquad\qquad\qquad\qquad ab = 6 \times 3 = 18$

$\dfrac{a}{b} = a \div b$ $\qquad\qquad\qquad\qquad \dfrac{a}{b} = 6 \div 3 = 2$

$2a = 2 \times a$ $\qquad\qquad\qquad\qquad 2 \times a = 2 \times 6 = 12$
(Always write the number before the letter.)

1. **Find the totals.**

    a $\quad ab =$ _____ $\qquad\qquad a = 8 \qquad b = 9$

    b $\quad 2c - 1 =$ _____ $\qquad c = 10$

    c $\quad 5t + 6 =$ _____ $\qquad t = 7$

    d $\quad \dfrac{n}{m} + 2 =$ _____ $\qquad n = 32 \qquad m = 8$

    e $\quad ab + \dfrac{a}{b} =$ _____ $\qquad a = 10 \qquad b = 5$

    f $\quad 4m - 2n =$ _____ $\qquad m = 7 \qquad n = 6$

    g $\quad \dfrac{c}{d} + 10 =$ _____ $\qquad c = 100 \qquad d = 20$

    h $\quad 6h + 33 =$ _____ $\qquad h = 11$

    i $\quad 7n + 21 =$ _____ $\qquad n = 3$

2. **Find the value of each letter.**

    a $\quad 5a = 10 \qquad = 5 \times ? = 10 \qquad a =$ _____

    b $\quad 4b - 2 = 10 = 4 \times ? - 2 = 10 \qquad b =$ _____

    c $\quad 3m + 5 = 23 = 3 \times ? + 5 = 23 \qquad m =$ _____

    d $\quad 6c = 42 \qquad\qquad\qquad\qquad\qquad c =$ _____

    e $\quad 3t - 15 = 15 \qquad\qquad\qquad\quad t =$ _____

    f $\quad 20b + 8 = 48 \qquad\qquad\qquad\quad b =$ _____

Sometimes you need to find **a rule for a number sequence** that helps you find not only the next answer in the sequence but, say, the 54th or 78th number (term).

To find the value of any term in a sequence we use the *n*th term rule.
(*n* stands for the number of the term you are looking for)

Look at this sequence.

2 4 6 8 10 12 14 16
In this sequence 2 is added each time.
Therefore the *n*th term = 2 × *n* = 2*n*

So, if we wanted to find the 54th number in this sequence …

$$n\text{th term} = 2n$$
$$54\text{th term} = 2 \times 54$$
$$= 108$$

3. **Find the *n*th term for each of these sequences.**

   a 3   6   9   12   15   18   *n*th term = _____

   b 5   10   15   20   25   30   *n*th term = _____

   c 7   14   21   28   35   42   *n*th term = _____

   d 10   20   30   40   50   60   *n*th term = _____

   e 4   8   12   16   20   24   *n*th term = _____

4. **Use the *n*th term rules to find the given term.**

   a *n*th term = 4*n*   **b** *n*th term = 8*n*
      35th term = _____   22nd term = _____

   c *n*th term = 2*n*   **d** *n*th term = 5*n*
      97th term = _____   15th term = _____

Tough	OK	Got it!

0   24

Total

24

Challenge yourself

Find the *n*th term for these sequences. You will need to think carefully!

   a 3   5   7   9   11   13   *n*th term = _____

   b 7   11   15   19   23   27   *n*th term = _____

Square, cube and triangular numbers

A **square number** is a number multiplied by itself.

It looks like a square!

A cube number is when a number is multiplied by itself three times. The calculation is written like this ...

$4 \times 4 = $ = $4^2 = 16$ $3^3 = 3 \times 3 \times 3 = 27$

1. **Fill in the gaps.**

    a $6 \times 6 = $ _____6^2_____ = _____36_____

    b $8 \times 8 = $ _____8^2_____ = _____

    c $5 \times 5 = $ _____ = _____

    d $2 \times 2 = $ _____ = _____

    e $9 \times 9 = $ _____ = _____

    f 12×12 _____ = _____

    g _____ = $7^2 = $ _____

    h _____ = $11^2 = $ _____

2. **Complete this number sequence of square numbers.**

1			16			49			100		

3. **Complete these cube numbers.**

    a $4 \times 4 \times 4 = $ ____ = ____^{3}

    b $2 \times 2 \times 2 = $ ____ = ____

    c $6 \times 6 \times 6 = $ ____ = ____

    d $9 \times 9 \times 9 = $ ____ = ____

    e $5 \times 5 \times 5 = $ ____ = ____

    f $7 \times 7 \times 7 = $ ____ = ____

4. **Complete this number sequence for cube numbers.**

    1 _____ _____ 64 _____ _____ 343 _____ _____ _____

Just as a square number looks like a square, a triangular number looks like a triangle!

Triangular numbers

= 1   = 3   = 6

5. **Find the next four triangular numbers.**

1	3	6				

For your workings

6. **Write a rule for finding triangular numbers.**

_____

_____

0	Tough	OK	Got it! 17

Total

17

Challenge yourself

Look at the numbers below. They are either square or triangular numbers. Draw a triangle or square around each number to show which category they belong to.

169   45   120   225

Factors, multiples and prime numbers

Factors = numbers that **divide equally** into other numbers

Multiples = numbers that contain another number an **exact** number of times

1. **Ring the numbers in the box that are factors of ...**

a 10

| 6 | 2 | 7 | 5 | 3 | 10 |

b 20

| 4 | 17 | 8 | 5 | 10 | 6 |

c 36

| 9 | 2 | 13 | 7 | 18 | 15 |

d 62

| 1 | 5 | 2 | 12 | 6 | 31 |

e 54

| 9 | 8 | 29 | 3 | 27 | 6 |

2. **Ring the numbers in the box that are multiples of ...**

a 6

| 36 | 2 | 15 | 78 | 81 | 60 |

b 9

| 16 | 81 | 71 | 52 | 117 | 36 |

c 12

| 13 | 60 | 121 | 144 | 84 | 79 |

d 7

| 49 | 39 | 65 | 28 | 96 | 105 |

e 5

| 32 | 15 | 54 | 215 | 86 | 90 |

A **prime number** has only two factors:

1 and the number itself.

QUICK TIP!
1 is not a prime number as it only has one factor!

3. **On the 10 × 10 square, colour in all the prime numbers.**
The first two have been done for you.

0	1	2	3	4	5	6	7	8	9
10	11	12	13	14	15	16	17	18	19
20	21	22	23	24	25	26	27	28	29
30	31	32	33	34	35	36	37	38	39
40	41	42	43	44	45	46	47	48	49
50	51	52	53	54	55	56	57	58	59
60	61	62	63	64	65	66	67	68	69
70	71	72	73	74	75	76	77	78	79
80	81	82	83	84	85	86	87	88	89
90	91	92	93	94	95	96	97	98	99

Tough	OK	Got it!

0   11

Total 11

Challenge yourself

A line of counters is set out in a pattern.

2 white 3 coloured 2 white 3 coloured . . .

a   Is the 48th counter white or coloured? _____

b   What position in the line is the 14th coloured counter? _____

47

Estimation

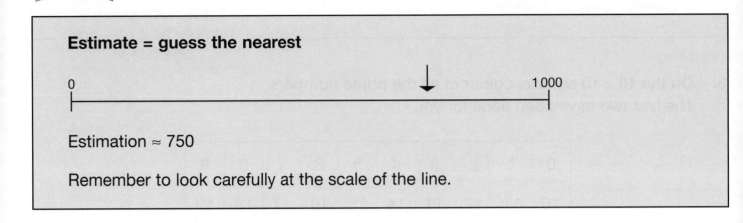

Estimate = guess the nearest

0   1 000

Estimation ≈ 750

Remember to look carefully at the scale of the line.

1. **Estimate the number that the arrow is pointing to.**

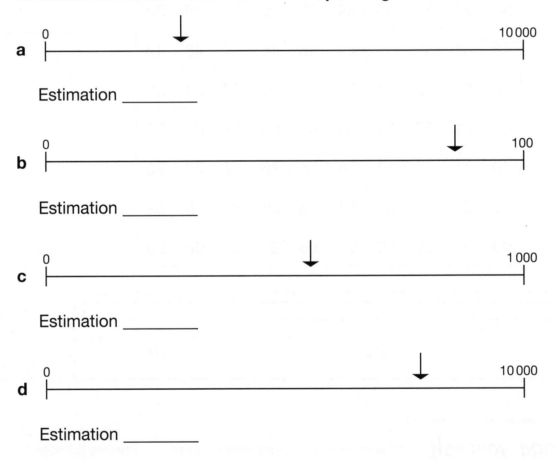

a

Estimation _____

b

Estimation _____

c

Estimation _____

d

Estimation _____

2. **Draw an arrow where you estimate these numbers will be on each of the number lines.**

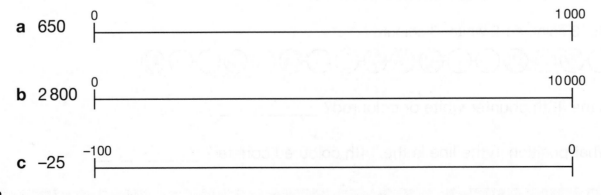

a 650

b 2 800

c −25

3. **Estimate the right answer to these problems.**

Show your workings. Use ≈ in your workings.

QUICK TIP!
≈ is the same as writing 'is approximately equal to'

a Estimate how many penny coins will make a straight line 1 m long. _____

b Estimate how many bricks there are in a wall of your house. _____

c Estimate how many loaves of bread your family will eat during 10 years. _____

d Estimate how many leaves are on a tree near your house. _____

For your workings

Tough	OK	Got it!

0   11

Total

/11

Challenge yourself

If you had 1 300 000 seconds, which of these would you be able to do?

- Spend one week on holiday

- Spend ten days in Spain

- Spend a fortnight skiing

- Spend a month on a holiday cruise

- Spend a year going around the world

Explain how you decided.

_____

_____

Ratio and proportion

Ratio describes the relationship between two things.

You make a jug of juice for some friends.
The ratio of juice to water for the drink is …
1 glass of juice **to every** 4 glasses of water.
Ratio = 1 : 4

The **proportion** (fraction) of juice is $\frac{1}{5}$.

1. **Write the ratio of black squares to white squares in each of these patterns.**

a

__1__ to every __3__   Ratio = 1 : 3

b

____ to every ____   Ratio = ____ : ____

c

____ to every ____   Ratio = ____ : ____

d

____ to every ____   Ratio = ____ : ____

e

____ to every ____   Ratio = ____ : ____

f

____ to every ____   Ratio = ____ : ____

2. Now write the number of black squares as a fraction of the total in each of the patterns in 1.

a $\frac{1}{4}$

b _____

c _____

d _____

e _____

f _____

3. Solve these problems.

a There are two girls for every three boys watching a school football match. 30 children are watching the match.

How many girls are watching? _____

b There is a plate of 24 cakes. Caleb eats one in every four cakes.

How many cakes does he eat? _____

c Mr Bevan has 40 fish in his pond. A stork eats two in every five of his fish.

How many fish does the stork eat? _____

d A joint of beef needs to be cooked for 40 minutes for every kg.

How long does a $3\frac{1}{2}$ kg joint of beef take to cook? _____

| 0 | Tough | OK | Got it! | 14 |

Total

/ 14

Challenge yourself

Look at these shapes.
Describe in terms of ratio and proportion the relationship between the two shapes.

_____

_____

_____

Perimeter and area

Perimeter = the distance around the outside edge of a shape
Area = the space inside a 2D shape

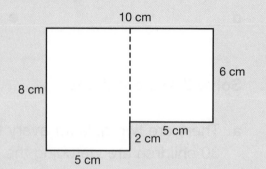

Look carefully at this shape.

Perimeter = 10 cm + 6 cm + 5 cm + 2 cm + 5 cm + 8 cm = 36 cm

It is easier to find the **area** if we split the shape into two rectangles.
Remember, **area = base × height**

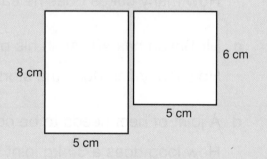

Area = $(8 \times 5) + (6 \times 5)$
$40 \text{ cm}^2 + 30 \text{ cm}^2 = 70 \text{ cm}^2$

1. **Find the perimeter and area of these shapes.**

   a

   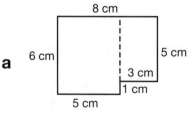

   Perimeter =
   Area =

   b

   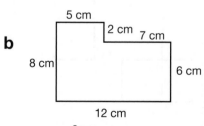

   Perimeter =
   Area =

   c

   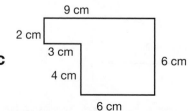

   Perimeter =
   Area =

To find the **area of this right-angled triangle** we need to find the area of the rectangle first.

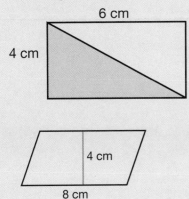

6 cm

4 cm

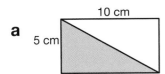

4 cm

8 cm

Area of rectangle = base × height
= 6 × 4 = 24 cm^2

Area of triangle = $\frac{1}{2}$ base × height
= $\frac{1}{2}$ of 6 × 4
= $\frac{1}{2}$ of 24 cm^2
= 12 cm^2

Area of parallelogram = base × height
= 8 × 4
= 32 cm^2

2. **Find the area of these triangles.**

a
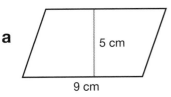
10 cm
5 cm

Area of rectangle = _____
Area of triangle = _____

b
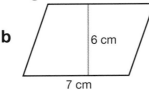
7 cm
4 cm

Area of rectangle = _____
Area of triangle = _____

c
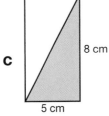
8 cm
5 cm

Area of rectangle = _____
Area of triangle = _____

3. **Find the area of these parallelograms.**

a
5 cm
9 cm

Area = _____

b
6 cm
7 cm

Area = _____

c
3 cm
8 cm

Area = _____

0
Tough   OK   Got it!
9

Total

9

Challenge yourself

A rectangle has an area of 24 cm^2.
List four different perimeters this rectangle might have.

_____   _____

_____   _____

Another rectangle has an area of 36 cm^2. How many different perimeters can this rectangle have? _____

Angles

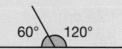
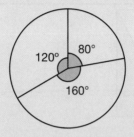
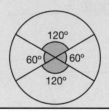
1. **Find the missing angles.**

a

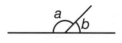

a = 135°

b = _____

b

a = 25°

b = 55°

c = _____

c

a = 57°

b = _____

d

a = 72°

b = _____

e

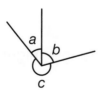

a = 40°

b = 75°

c = _____

f

a = 88°

b = _____

Angles inside a triangle always add up to **180°**.

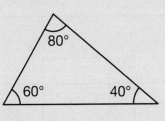

80°

60°   40°

60° + 40° + 80° = 180°

Angles inside a quadrilateral always add up to **360°**.

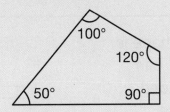

100°

120°

50°   90°

50° + 90° + 120° + 100° = 360°

2.   **Find the missing angles.**

a

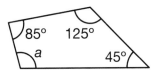

85°   125°

a

45°

a = _____

b

66°

a   34°

a = _____

c

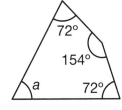

72°

154°

a   72°

a = _____

Total

0   9

Tough   OK   Got it!

9

Challenge yourself

Draw the following shapes:

a   a triangle with three angles of 60° and sides measuring 5 cm.

b   a quadrilateral with four angles, two measuring 80° and two measuring 100°, and each side measuring 4 cm.

Shapes

The **net** of a 3D shape is the 2D shape that can be cut out and folded up into a 3D shape.

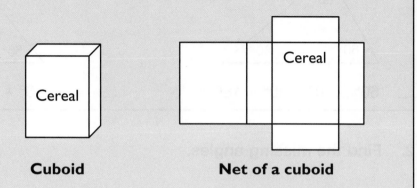

Cuboid   **Net of a cuboid**

1. **Draw a net for each of these shapes.**

a

b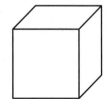

c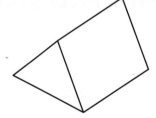

2. **Name the 3D shapes in 1.**

a _____ b _____ c _____

All these definitions are labels of measure for a **circle**.

radius = the distance from the centre of a circle to any point on the circumference
diameter = the distance across a circle, through the centre
circumference = the perimeter of a circle

3. **Label the radius, diameter and circumference on this circle.**

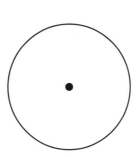

4. **With a line, match each of these 2D shapes with its name.**

a    b    c    d

scalene triangle   trapezium   kite   parallelogram

Tough	OK	Got it!

0   11

Total

/11

Challenge yourself

Write a description for each of the shapes in question 4, without naming the shape.

a kite _____

b trapezium _____

c scalene triangle _____

d parallelogram _____

Check your definitions in a dictionary.
Now, without giving away the name of the shape, read your description to someone.
Can they name the shape?

Volume

Volume is the amount of space in a 3D shape.

It is measured in cubic units, e.g. cm^3, m^3

You can find the volume of a shape by counting how many unit cubes fit inside it.

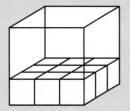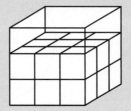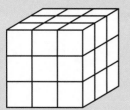

These cuboids are being filled with $1\,cm^3$ cubes.

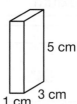

1. **How many $1\,cm^3$ cubes would you need to fill these shapes?**

a
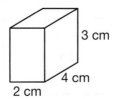
3 cm
4 cm
2 cm

Volume = _____ cm^3

b
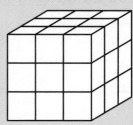
5 cm
3 cm
1 cm

Volume = _____ cm^3

c
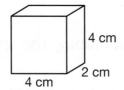
4 cm
2 cm
4 cm

Volume = _____ cm^3

d
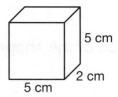
5 cm
2 cm
5 cm

Volume = _____ cm^3

e
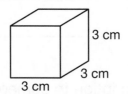
3 cm
3 cm
3 cm

Volume = _____ cm^3

f
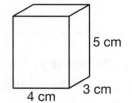
5 cm
3 cm
4 cm

Volume = _____ cm^3

There is an easy rule to work out the volume of a cuboid.

Volume = length × width × height (V = l × w × h)

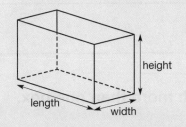

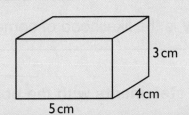

The volume of this cuboid = length × width × height
= 5 cm × 4 cm × 3 cm
= 60 cm³

2. **Find the volume of these cubes.**

a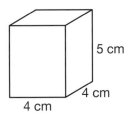

5 cm
4 cm
4 cm

Volume = _____ cm³

b

8 cm
6 cm
2 cm

Volume = _____ cm³

c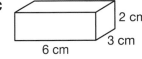

2 cm
3 cm
6 cm

Volume = _____ cm³

d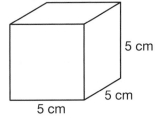

5 cm
5 cm
5 cm

Volume = _____ cm³

e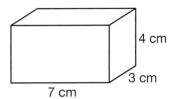

4 cm
3 cm
7 cm

Volume = _____ cm³

f

4 cm
18 cm
1 cm

Volume = _____ cm³

0			12
Tough	OK	Got it!	

Total

12

Challenge yourself

Find the height of each of these cubes.

a Volume = 27 cm³

Height = _____ cm

b Volume = 216 cm³

Height = _____ cm

c Volume = 512 cm³

Height = _____ cm

Probability

Probability is the likelihood of something happening.

1. **Match the statements with the boxes. Some may link with more than one box.**

   a I will eat breakfast in the morning ●

   b It will get dark at night ●

   c I will see the Queen tomorrow ●

   d It will rain on my birthday ●

   e I will stand on the moon next week ●

   f I will eat a bag of crisps at the weekend ●

   g I will talk to a friend tonight ●

   ● CERTAIN

   ● LIKELY

   ● UNLIKELY

   ● IMPOSSIBLE

   ● POSSIBLE

2. **Read the example and list two more events that can have only two possible outcomes.**

   The new baby will be a boy or a girl.

   _____

   _____

3. **List two events that have only one possible outcome.**

   _____

   _____

Challenge yourself

Answer the questions below by conducting your own experiment.

How many times do you need to throw a dice to get a 6?

Make a note of the number of times you need to throw a dice to get a 6. Do this 15 times.

Fill in the table.

Experiment	No. of throws to get a 6
1	
2	
3	
4	
5	
6	
7	
8	
9	
10	
11	
12	
13	
14	
15	

Look at the table above.

What is the probability of throwing a 6 …

a on the first throw? _____

b on the third throw? _____

c on the sixth throw? _____

d on the tenth throw? _____

How am I doing?

1. Find the totals.

    a $5n + 69 =$ _____ $n = 10$ **b** $3b - 12 =$ _____ $b = 15$

2. Write two square and two triangular numbers greater than the number 17.

square numbers   [ ]   [ ]

triangular numbers   [ ]   [ ]

3. Ring the numbers in the box that are factors of ...

    a 15 | 7   11   5   14   3   21 |

    b 30 | 15   3   5   2   6   10 |

    c 84 | 2   10   7   42   12   15 |

4. Draw an arrow where you estimate the number will be on the number line.

    a 28   0 ————————————————————— 100

    b 650   0 ————————————————————— 1 000

    c 2 800   0 ————————————————————— 10 000

5. Write the ratio and proportion of black squares to white squares.

ratio = _____ : _____   proportion = _____

6. **Find the perimeter and area of this shape.**

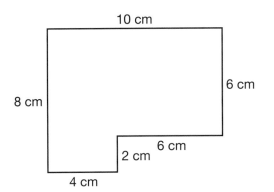

perimeter = _____

area = _____

7. **Fill in the missing angle:**

a

65

_____ °

b
110

_____ °

8. **Label the radius, diameter and circumference on this circle.**

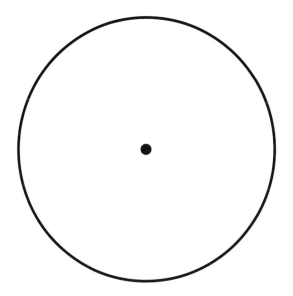

9. **Write a statement where the probability of something happening is UNLIKELY.**

_____

_____

Total

15

63

10–11 years assessment

1. Find the total of 32·6, 63·2 and 125. _____

2. What is a prime number?

   _____

3. Write the percentage.   **a** 1·0 = _____%   **b** 0·5 = _____%

4. Write the mode and median of these numbers.

   6   7   1   3   9   6   1   2   6

   Mode = _____   Median = _____

5. The temperature is −7 °C. How much does it rise to reach 8 °C? _____

6. Divide 506 by 23. _____

7. Look at the number sentences. The first is correct; is the second?

   $36 \times 45 = 1620$ $1620 \div 45 = 37$

8. How many eighths in $3\frac{5}{8}$? _____

9. Complete this number sentence. $4\cdot8 \times 6 =$ _____

10. Is 462 divisible by 3?   Yes / No

11. Change this improper fraction to a mixed number. $\frac{50}{8} =$ _____

12. Put these numbers in order, largest first.

    2·78   2·87   0·278   2·278   2·287

    _____   _____   _____   _____   _____

13. Write the following to one decimal place.

    a 8·92 _____   **b** 12·831 _____   **c** 333·333 _____

14. Multiply 442 by 28. _____

15. If the nth term = 6n, what is the 23rd term? _____

64